STARCHILD

BY

IZZI TETTERTON

COPYRIGHT © 2019 IZZI TETTERTON

ALL RIGHTS RESERVED.

ISBN: 9781092214056

DEDICATION

Dedicated to my mothers;
The one who roams the Earth, the one who is the Earth,
the one who lights the sky, and all the ones who sparkle
in the dark.

Thank you for your inspiration.

CONTENTS

Star Child	1
Strawberry Girl	2
The Emperor's Words	3
Silver	4
Afflatus	5
My Darling	6
Scarlet	7
Obsession of Lust	8
The Fool (Alpha)	9
The Creator	10
Extrasolar Lover	11
Addict	12
The Ocean	13
Thicker Than Water	14
Potent	15
Holy Child	16
French Quarter	17
The Magician	18

Death of the Illusion	19
The Tower	20
Despondency	21
Passage of Time	22
Desolate	23
Judas Kiss	24
Changing of the Season	25
The Desert Sun	26
Existence	27
Purgatory	28
Desolation	29
The Towns of Sorrow and Perturbation	31
The Art of Suicide	32
The Hermit	33
The Moon	34
Rain	35
Ashen	36
The Prodigy	37
The Lovers	38
Psychedelia Babe	39

Lovely Chaos	40
Dragon Lady	41
Ace of Rods	42
La Douleur Exquise	43
Soulmate	44
A Moment	45
The Wanderer	46
Page of Rods	47
The Fool (Omega)	48
Escape Society	49
Serenity	50
Flower Child	51

ACKNOWLEDGMENTS

I would like to give special thanks to my sister, Madeline, who not only helped edit this book but also listened to me read her these poems over and over and over again.
Thank you for believing in and encouraging me, I couldn't have done it without you.

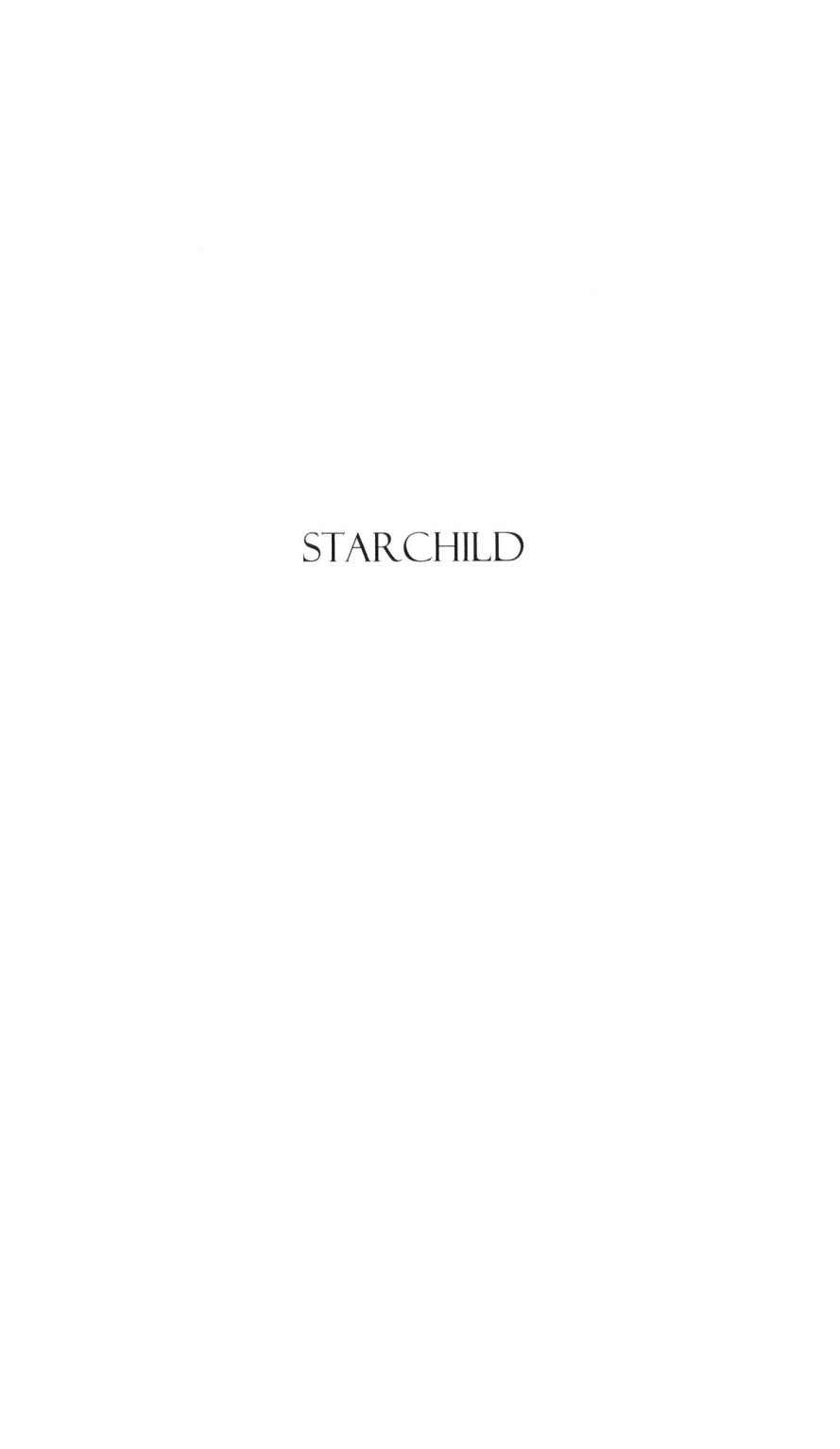

STARCHILD

STAR CHILD

A flower she blooms to her fullest.
Delicate, sacred, divine.

Desired by all,
envied by many,
cherished truly by few.

But a flower she is not,
for in her heart lay
a boiling rage of excitement.

She is a diamond
crushed by the pressure of being a flower,
hardened by disbelief,
and created to shine
in comparison to no others.

STRAWBERRY GIRL

Red taints the soulless dame,
so she often hides away.

Dye stains her spotted skin
with brown and blonde and tan.
Some to cover up the "evil"
and others to hide the snowy glow,
that's determined to make her stay
some awful ghost.

A fetish.
They get their kicks
and mock her for her ways,
then knock her down again
just because they can.

A slave, unworthy,
the bottom of the pit.
But such is how it is,
for a woman painted red.

THE EMPEROR'S WORDS

My star,
my beautiful little star;
how you shine so bright
and love so hard.

Enchanting your spell to tease me,
you steal my soul
with your flourishing life.

Raped by my demons,
healed with my kiss
that I place against your angel lips.

You are a veil of flickering light,
wrapped around my encased fire;
urging me to do what I do.

SILVER

As he ages, like a raisin;
the wrinkles do come,
but the older the sweeter,
for more knowledge is contained,
inside his delightfully wicked, old brain.

AFFLATUS

My beautiful muse
you steal the air from my lungs,
making me breathless.

MY DARLING

My darling,
your lips are like a symphony
swirling magic through the air.
Your body is like a lullaby,
moving lovingly around my build.

Your soul sings to the melody,
of a God's design
and your hands they play upon the earth,
dancing through the sky.

My darling, your eyes are like portals
to a different world,
and your mind, a sage
creating beauty everywhere you turn.

My darling, you are perfection
in each and every flaw.

My darling,
you are poetry,
stealing away my heart.

SCARLET

Kissed softly, tender to the touch,
blossoming by the second,
almost to erupt.

Joyous gift of maturity
skips playfully through your bones,
and to my ears you call my name,
often times I come.

Skin so ravished, blotted red,
heated up to my cheeks,
filled with all your sins,
that now flow deep in me.

OBSESSION OF LUST

I want to wander
amongst your savage thoughts
and lose myself in your primitive lips.

Let me touch your inner most soul
and take you on a journey into a place
where the rhythm of our heartbeats intertwine.

Let me ignite your passion
and devour your fears.

For I am the sapid taste
on your tongue
and the radical movements on your hips.

THE FOOL (ALPHA)

There is a novelty that comes with knowing you,
more precious than all time.

The intimate secrets you share with me
are sacred to my mind,
but not for me to prove our love
or boast about the world.

But because with each and everything,
I fall deeper and deeper in love.

THE CREATOR

Adrenaline manhandles
each assessment of his work,
boyishly ravishing like it's his first.

Exerting such command
as he beats away, dominating veins
that scream of joy and pleasure
through every thought he makes.

Sip, sip, sip down to the pit,
coffee feeding
the already sickened brain.
Ideas run in his giddy sweat
that drip into his pen.

Expelling such compelling work,
but deeming it as no good.
Until a masterpiece unravels,
the maestro will not stop his work.

EXTRASOLAR LOVER

My soul longs to tame the cloud
that hangs around your face.
But you are so distant; always getting carried away.
In the stars, your mind is trapped, so very high in space,
so I will try to grab your feet
and bring you back down to reality.

An anxious muse you are, and me- a silly girl,
but for a second if I could lift my arms,
I would pull our bodies close and cling your lips to mine.

If thoughts could tell stories,
how yours would write so well;
but harsh with words you can often be,
never conveying them well.

So speak to me through life, with kisses on my cheeks.
Tell me what you want to say while making love to me,
and I will write you poetry, or paint you in your room,
take your picture on a polaroid; as to not disturb you.

ADDICT

Dark purple marks linger on my chest,
dancing up and around my neckline.

A shaky feeling of fear and fantasy
skip through my mind.
I hear you creep into the room,
swiftly moving over me
like the shadows playing in the streets.

A man as dark as you
should not control my brain,
but I ache for the drug
that pulsates through your veins.

THE OCEAN

Mother warms the Earth,
you soften her blow with your cool embrace
crashing against my heated skin.

I am a star child
caught between the radiant glow of my mother
and the whispers of your voice;
luring me to sleep in a seemingly endless lullaby.

When my mother isn't looking,
you come to play the most,
creeping up further without fear of being seen.
Your body sprinkles on me
like the stars in the sky.

Although you are an everlasting journey
of scary new things, I call you friend.
Lost in your blue-green serenity,
struck with your violent grey marks;
I am at home inside your twisted ways.

THICKER THAN WATER

A bond more powerful than one of lust,
covered in thorns and years of blood;
cured over, dried out;
from painful stabbing through the soul.

My heart grew solid from anger and rage-
inside a gooey yolk remains,
reminding my brain just what sweet memories
we did make.

The tears swell up
then fall from my eyes,
just as they did before you sang a lullaby.

But that sword still pressing on,
and the blood still drips,
and the wound not scarred.

A goodbye more painful than the wound itself,
but a goodbye I must say.
So that someday, we might have a better life.

POTENT

I am taken by
intense and dramatic love
that consumes my soul.

HOLY CHILD

On her knees where her lord is watching
soft cries fall from her eyes.
Filled with pleasure.

She grips the bed sheets
as her nails tear the spread,
like her lips to his touch.

FRENCH QUARTER

Learning more with every glance,
who's the man behind the mask.
Hiding away, you keep your graces,
but a flashy friend reveals your faces.

New to me, but drives me wild,
a feeling like those of a child.

Sparkles entangled in your smile
revealing to me your true style.
Under the fever of the lights,
jiving through the night,
we dance along
with New Orleans's street life.

THE MAGICIAN

The shell of a man he used to be.
Once a beacon of power and plays
now he sits dying of old age.

A fine specimen of man,
we all did know,
now crumbles before mortalities blow.

And we wait,
while his character evolves,
to find out if the rumors are false,
but alas secrets still kept
he'll take to the grave.

An illustrious illusion still hazes the way,
and for now he is safe, in his tower,
locked away.

DEATH OF THE ILLUSION

I am a flower planted in the dry heat,
flourishing in the most extreme conditions.
I get love from every drop of rain.
Helping me to grow,
It heals my soul and replenishes me,
preparing me for the next brutal beating.

THE TOWER

Can't sleep, filled with angst,
racing, pacing in my brain.

How do I rest when the covers of my eyes
refuse their warm embrace,
straying from the dreams that sanctuate and tame.

Did I betray my mind
with thoughts of days that remain?
Keeping it from reminiscing with its love of tender sleep.

Please forgive me
from straying from my calming breath,
and carry on romancing darkness's sweet kiss.

DESPONDENCY

I see my reflection and think:
this is who I'll always be.
But the universe knows better.
Soon, my life will be
just another collection of old stories.

PASSAGE OF TIME

Growing from a sapling
into a beautiful flower
then wilting away.

A journey all must take,
giving bits of our soul along the way,
to those who wandered in
and asked to stay.

Breaking off pieces
until none were left.
Gone to the beings
who we loved the most;

Now gone,
we too must go.

DESOLATE

Heart torn from my chest,
feeling nothingness in me.
Numbness consumes all.

JUDAS KISS

Vast Abyss;
numb feeling of nothingness.

A pit upon my soul,
that makes my heart so inhospitably cold;
not to be warmed by the shaking of my betrayed body.

Upset,
beyond the point of sickness.
Trembling,
in disbelief.

Tears come with a passionate thrust against my chest
hoping to force me from this still state.

I sit in agonizing pain,
gasping;
but no air sets me free.

A loss so severe,
trapping me in my motionless mind.

I am destroyed,
by one I hold near.

CHANGING OF THE SEASON

Autumn leaves fall in much dismay,
raped the ground with promises made.
Hope does splinter by the thread,
all that's good will soon be dead.

THE DESERT SUN

Sift into the sand,
to bury away the cries of my splintered skin.
Ounce by ounce freckled by the glare.

The dunes fall to the ends of time,
trapping those who dare to look
further than you care.

Leave me to weep in the wicked heat-
blistered, red from all your beatings

Rays they spy, tears they dry
all from the heat of the desert sky.

EXISTENCE

Dust to dust we crumble.
Stillness prevails.
A story fails to tell its tale.
The absolute is everywhere.

PURGATORY

My heart weighs so heavy inside my chest
and yet the pressure does not draw
a single tear upon my flesh.

Liberate me, sweet jaws of death,
or forever I remain in life's merciless debt.

DESOLATION

Filling my soul is a feeling
so allusive to myself,
not even the dark matter of the universe
would suffice to fill the role.

It consumes my body
creating a void of suffering,
erupting in my stomach's pit,
wrapping around my heart
only to expand in my chest,
leaving me winded.

A storm upon the sea,
where my body is frozen
in icy cold thoughts.

Dead eyes,
pierce through a spot on the wall,
leaving my mouth hanging open
in a dull state.

An agonizing lust,
taunts me to move
but not a single limb listens.

I twitch in silence.
While my head is screaming,
lips remain still,
as if they have nothing to say.

Isolated
to the confines of this ever-tiny cell
I urge myself to escape to death.

THE TOWNS OF SORROW AND PERTURBATION

Two towns, she lives in both.
One is dark and black; the sun never rises,
the moon doesn't shine.
The people in this town don't go outside;
but she does.
And when she does she stands alone;
stalked by the shadows of the hiding town folk.

In the other town
everyone knows all,
but they are not her friends.
They talk to her always,
their voices drain everything out.
The sun beats down on her
and there is no night to ease the heat.

Her only relief is the numbness of her mind,
which aids her every day
when she is forced to walk through both.
Her only hope is to find a place
where night and day preside
and equal is the way of life.

THE ART OF SUICIDE

Longing for the one I love, yet,
the only companion I find
is one so cold and sharp against my flesh;
slicing into the loneliness.

Beauty bleeds into the Earth,
with every drop of blood.
Wasted time seeps the velvet dress,
parading darkness around my gasping chest.
Tears, they trickle down my cheeks,
soft with fading pink.

My anger turns to sorrow,
and my sorrows to goodbyes,
but even in my death
the love for you will never die.

Suicide is never the answer.
The things you are going through may be hard now, but in the future, it will get better.
Please get help if you are depressed or suicidal.

THE HERMIT

The older I become, the more I recede,
for I realize surface layer conversations
are just not quite for me.

Smiles often greeting, but those are mostly fake,
the personal gain from the bragging game
is really not my favorite take.

I appreciate solitarity;
the exclusiveness of my mind,
being completely alone with just my thoughts
is where I'd like to spend my time.

THE MOON

Creature of darkness
rising from the deepest state of somber,
I heed your calls.

Creep onto my body whilst I sleep,
pounding heavily
into my interrupted dreams.

Bags dragging on the floor,
weeping from the pain.
And at last I drown my sorrows.

Be gone!

Ugly beast,
who wastes poor innocent souls,
let me slip out of my mind,
for this time, life has won.

RAIN

If my life were a movie,
I'd understand the rain;
especially when tears are paired
with events, dramatic and strange.

You see if my existence meant something,
then the rain knows when to come.
Like when I need a good night's sleep,
or when I need to just not think.
The rain climbs as emotions peak,
as if I'm in some scene.

The universe must surely know me,
because if not I can't seem to understand why
the rain knows just when I need it to come.

ASHEN

Born of a God
stretching down to Earth,
body stained by soil
planting love of life.

A hidden soul escaping away,
to secrete his thoughts of grief.
The only sentient being in this gloomy world,
watching billions waste away
as he burns to ash.

THE PRODIGY

Kisses of splendid love upon his slim bare chest;
the hair tickles my glossed-over lips,
sending giggles surging through with every single breath.
He smiles that charming smile,
and ever so smitten I become.
A truly holy man is what I've come to love!

THE LOVERS

Body baking in the warm sun.
Always being the one to retreat;
I now lay exposed in your arms.

The most intense form of intimacy
is the kind I experience
while talking to you.

PSYCHEDELIA BABE

Goddess chick,
passing off such groovy vibes.
Lighting up my karma;
in full desire
it sets fire.

LOVELY CHAOS

French bounces off her tongue
like the cigarette that hits her lips.
A smile pops the side of her face
as she takes a nice long drag.

Catching a glimpse of her sad eyes
pulls me deep into her trance;
leaving me to question
the sanity of our dark, twisted romance.

Poised tits,
pointing up to the heavens,
as if to taunt the angels
who've banished her to hell.
But for now, her and her fantastic sins
will dance around the Earth
wreaking havoc all around.

DRAGON LADY

Temptress with the fiery hair,
onto men you seduce ideas.
Sweet like red wine;
but much like the juice of the grape,
a tantrum, too, brews in you.

Ride your chariot home,
through the dancing devil's parade.
To the music, plot
all your sinful games.

Play your tricks like the
man who plays guitars,
you play as well as he does
but now upon his heart.

ACE OF RODS

The change might not come sudden;
but overtime
like a dandelion blowing with the breeze
what has been,
will no longer be.

Right now I am scattered in petals;
broken and torn.
But the wind dries my tears
and shushes me to sleep;
leaving me dreaming
of the sweetness
that will soon become of me.

LA DOULEUR EXQUISE

Alluring soul
inducing such persuasive thoughts.

To spend an eternity chasing
would be a waste;
considering a spirit as intent
on existing as it's grown to be,
could not at this time flourish with me.

Lovers no doubt, just not meant to be.
Now must continue on searching
for their everlasting.

SOULMATE

I'm up all night thinking
how my love is oh-so far.
But in my dreams I see him,
like how I see the stars.
He's there,
I just can't hold him
or love him like I want.
But if I speak to him aloud,
he hears it in his heart.

Dedicated to the future love of my life and my Grandparents:
Marshall and Dianne. May I have a love as strong as theirs.
RIP Grandpa, 1945-2018

A MOMENT

The thing about a moment is,
that when it passes, it's forever gone.
In that moment we don't see
how quickly things become memories.
The thing about this moment was,
I could spend an eternity
reminiscing just the thought.

THE WANDERER

No matter where I go,
no place quite feels like home.
As time keeps passing on,
I feel that in my heart,
I don't belong right here.

I'm not sure I belong quite anywhere.

Perhaps amongst the stars
is the place that holds my heart.
Perhaps I'm just a traveler,
merely making stops to recollect my thoughts.

I wander along the concrete roads,
seldom taking flight.
But no matter where I am right now,
it's never really right.

Dedicated to my Papa.

PAGE OF RODS

Looking up towards the heavens
my soul's comfort comes from the flickering stars
sprinkling down upon my flesh.
I am dreaming of sunlight's kiss,
waking me from my slumber.

RISE!
To the wind and the rain.
But blessed be the day I rejoice in.

THE FOOL (OMEGA)

Setting my soul upon a goal
as unattainable as it is to touch the sun.

It is hard to be a dreamer
in a world so wound in time;
bounded in such hate and confusion.
It's easy to lose sight of all that is love.

That pestering urge telling me to listen
skips into my brain.
And when I stop,
I hear the music of my mother
whistle through the trees.

Letting the energy flow in
I go forward creating little harm.
For this, the universe repays,
my karma good, so good comes my way.

As unattainable as it seemed to be,
the sun beams now graze my skin,
setting me free.

ESCAPE SOCIETY

Off on an adventure I go,
sorry to inconvenience those
whose roots are so far tangled in with hate,
that they see me living in a dream-like state
and try to taint me with their wicked ways.

I let my soul's light guide the way and brighten the sky,
dimmed from my neglecting days.
Here amongst the clouds I feel alive
and the fear that trembled on my skin
can no longer reside in my life.

SERENITY

Sewing flowers into crowns
as they blossom all around,
so does peace and peace of mind,
for when I die, a flower will appear
in the Earth, above the place I lye.

FLOWER CHILD

You can find me where the water meets the land
or where the land meets the sky.
If all else fails, you can find me in a different world
full of vibrant life.

I live with my head cradled by the stars.
My existence isn't real, though neither are my thoughts.
But when I dance barefoot, naked in this realm,
I feel as if my soul is as real as it gets.

I go forth trekking places,
new and far and wide.
To find myself,
I suppose,
lost in this wilderness I grow so exposed.

I strip for the sake of nudity,
and make love for the sake of art.
My sweet lovers body,
I caress for the sake of pure dalliance.

Where there's music I will go,
where there's flowers I will grow.
Being the one who runs through fields of grass,

happily bouncing from the energy of the Earth's romance.

I am driven to live by a dream I once had,
as a child of the flowers upon this precious land.

AUTHOR'S NOTE

These poems are here to tell a story and express real emotion, in no-way are any of the poems aimed at romanticizing mental illnesses or suicide. *The Art of Suicide* was written as a reflection of a suicidal thought and was put into this book to convey despair and continue the story. If you are suicidal, depressed, or mentally ill please seek medical help. You matter and the world wouldn't be the same without you.

Thank you for reading *STARCHILD*, I truly hope you've enjoyed.

Much love and many blessings,
Izzi.

Made in the USA
Columbia, SC
25 May 2019